JOY COMETH IN THE MORNING

Prose, Short Stories And Paintings

James Cools Chambers

ACKNOWLEDGMENTS

All those who contributed to the publishing of this book are greatly appreciated, including the typist, editors, family, friends, and consultants whose untiring dedication contributed to its completeness.

May the words and paintings in this book bring smiles and joy to readers.

DEDICATION

This book is dedicated to that Divine Cause and giver of life.

TABLE OF CONTENTS

FOREWORD

Over the years, I have observed how much joy James experiences when sharing his ideas and thoughts with others. We met when he first started writing, and James was always so enthusiastic and eager to share. He also has a deep desire to paint, although for a long time he focused on paper sketches. One day out of the blue James was motivated to paint. He enrolled in a local art class, purchased his canvas, paints, brushes and other equipment and has been painting ever since.

It means so much to me to see him finally get a book of his stories and art work into print. Some stories are funny, others are thought provoking and challenging. It is my sincere desire that you enjoy James' works as much as I enjoy them.

Eloise Chambers

Tamarac, FL

March 2016

INTRODUCTION

The desire to write poems as a boy growing up on the island of Montserrat, whose capital is Plymouth, West Indies, was always there. When the poems presented themselves, I wrote them down, and most of the time I gave them away. I never put any value on what I wrote, especially when they were given to me freely by Mother Nature.

I am fortunate to have grown up on the Island of Montserrat with its beautiful hills, valleys, hot springs, an array of animals and multitude of plants and fruit trees. Montserrat is so beautiful that it is called the Emerald Isle of the West. Although, half of the island was destroyed by the Soufriere Hills Volcano in 1995, it remains peaceful and enchanting.

JOY COMETH IN THE MORNING

When I met my wife, Eloise, I started writing poems to her, and she encouraged me. Then I noticed that the poems or stories were present inside and outside of me. After reading some of my poems, fellow students in my art painting class suggested that I create a book. Here it is!

The title of the book, *Joy Cometh In The Morning: Prose, Short Stories And Paintings*, is appropriate to my experiences. To awake a conscious, living being with the blessing of health and the opportunity to continue growing and living a Dharmic life gives much joy.

It is my joy to walk early in the morning and I often play games with the Sun and nature, trying to see the changing colors of the Sun from a golden yellow to a shimmering silver color. I have not yet succeeded in observing this change. Imagine seeing the starry skies, the sounds of the birds and other animals, and the night turning into day. What a joyous experience! It is often after these quiet morning walks that the stories come.

CELEBRATION

(Rites of Passage)

Dear Yummy

Soon you will cross the threshold of adolescence and enter onto the world stage of life.

In your thoughts, you will be all alone, and the choices you make will be very important. So on your sixteenth birthday, start planning now for your future.

I want you to know that you have all the tools you need to be successful. Nothing but yourself can prevent you from being whatever you want to be.

As members of a minority group, education is our passport to success. As the saying goes, "A person's thoughts will make or break him or her."

I want you to know that I will always be thinking of you – wishing and hoping that you are doing fine.

Happy Birthday, Kurris

Maybe it was not easy to get to this birthday! But you persisted and traveled on, and now you can celebrate this birthday despite the challenges encountered.

Maybe sometimes you were disappointed and felt like giving up, but you were determined and continued to clear a path by removing some garbage in order to get to this birthday.

So now you can say, "Today is my birthday."

Happy Birthday!

Happy Birthday, Linda

Birthdays come around once a year to say hello and hoping you are happy and doing fine.

It comes to let you know you are still beautiful, loving, and kind, and that nothing in the world is like you.

"You are the soul; you are the Light Divine; you are loved; you are will, and you are wonderfully made."

As you awake from that deep sleep each morning you enjoy so much, may your heart be serene and filled with love and gratitude.

As the day progresses into night, may your heart be filled with that peace that brings liberation. Remember, you are never alone.

Happy Birthday, Linda, Again

Birthdays? How many? Interesting that the most miraculous was the first, the most precious. Were you invited? You came, but you had to wait for the most precious gift. Without it, you would not survive. What was that which you waited for?

When you got the gift, you sprang forth with a cry that welcomed you into this existence. Your cry was a joyous, happy cry. You brought lots of love with you because that is where you originated from, the pure love of the Creator, that which created all things.

Many who were there for this appearance were overcome with tears. There were very happy sounds. Everyone was happy to be there to welcome you.

Linda, as you celebrate this birthday, think about the happy experiences you have enjoyed on your life's journey, and give the God of your heart all the thanks you can give.

Happy Birthday to You.

Happy Mother's Day

There is something special about all mothers. They inherit the power of attraction and intuition.

When one reflects back on the first mother mentioned in one of the sacred texts of old, she is described as beautiful and fertile. The first mother was life; everything was in her.

Mothers of today, you are no different from the first mother, so, as you celebrate Mother's Day, remember that you are the microcosm of Mother Nature.

Through the centuries you have suffered and willfully been held in the shadow of men. Now, because of your persistence, will, and desire, you have broken the chains that kept you in what were only the appearances of the shadows. You now stand free in the light. You will go forth in time making the necessary change and adjustment, as you face the challenges of each day.

Soon, you will have the experience of impersonal (true) love that brings that inner peace that surpasses all understanding, the peace that we all crave.

When I think of my mother and how very special she was, I realize even though she is not with me today, she lives on forever in me. The same is true for you. As your children celebrate with you, you celebrate today within your mother.

Happy Mother's Day.

Oh, Mother

Oh, Mother of the earth, you will always be blessed.

The Absolute, the Creator of all things, and you, O Mother Earth, are about to become a procreator.

Be excited and be happy!

For you have become partners in life and death.

And remember you are special because all women are not fortunate to bring a life unto this earth.

Believe in yourself; that's all you need.

Love you.

DEATH

An Experience

The place was clean with spacious rooms decorated with paintings hanging on walls. People in the rooms were friendly but did not seem happy. They were there to celebrate the passing (transition) of a family member and friend. Most of those present knew the deceased and iterated many beautiful words about him. His sister spoke and said she loved her brother, although they had a rocky relationship at times. His son spoke about how his dad wrote poetry and how he tried to be a good son. There were many speeches, poetry, and songs.

The wife looked like all wives when their husband has passed on. She was sandwiched between two human comforters. We all have seen this scene many times in our lives; how sad it looked at the moment but that will change soon.

The deceased was special. He had two funeral services: a church ceremony and a Rosicrucian Memorial Ceremony.

The Rosicrucian Ceremony depicted our concept of transition (death) and was dramatically done. It brought a new experience to all of us. The deceased was a Rosicrucian member for over 50 years and was privileged even at death to share just a little of the Rosicrucian philosophy to family and friends in the most beautiful and eloquent way. Many of us left the ceremonies with mixed feelings and emotions, knowing that in the future we may have a similar experience.

Rosemary And Her Cats

Rosemary knew she was sick and dying. She had many cats and loved them passionately. They were her friends. She was always holding and caressing them and they showed their gratitude by purring and rubbing their bodies against her legs, face or other body parts.

There came a time when Rosemary got worse and too weak to move. The cats sensed something was not normal and would jump in her bed, lying peacefully, doing everything in their power to give her love and security. Yes, they were there for her, doing all that was possible, as if to comfort her. Even in her weakened condition, Rosemary was aware of her cats and did everything in her power to comfort them.

Finally, it was decided by Rosemary and her sisters that she should go to a hospice. The fateful hour came; Rosemary was being prepared to leave her house for the last time alive. As the process continued, the cats gathered and began to look at what was happening. They all had sad and curious looks on their faces. Intuitively, they knew it was the last time they would see Rosemary and felt the love that was so impersonal again. It was an indescribable moment. The cats were homeless, and there was no one to take care of them as Rosemary had. The hospice attendants placed Rosemary in the ambulance as the cats looked on. As the ambulance moved, the cats followed a short distance, knowing that it was only a moment of separation, a time to let go. Knowing deep down in their hearts that this separation was only temporary, they hoped Rosemary was at peace within and ready for her new life experience.

Was there a communication between Rosemary and her cats?

Rosemary Appleton Memorial

Brothers and Sisters,

There is no moment like now. I never dreamed that I would be standing in your presence to talk about Rosemary. I knew Rosemary for many years. We both were attracted to the Rosicrucian Philosophy, a Mystical Order.

Over the years, our friendship grew as we realized that we had many ideas in common. Rosemary studied and often talked about the Out of Body Experiences (OBE) she had. She even lectured on the subject. As Rosicrucians, we are very curious; we are told that we should be walking question marks and explore all aspects of life.

Rosemary was very versatile, and there was no challenge that would deter her. She used her hands as tools, not only to work on the computer where she earned her living but also to repair her roof and plumbing as well as doing other things that were needed.

Rosemary was an optimist. She was an uplifting human being of this world. She was loving, emphatic, and a peace-loving soul.

Rosemary, I imagine you have strived many years to find out who you are. There is a saying, "Man, know thyself." You knew death is only a transition; the body is a house and when the body cannot sustain the soul any longer, it goes back to Source, its creator.

I do hope you are prepared for that celestial spiritual home your soul had longed for all these years. Most of all, I wish you that peace that passeth all understanding. May you rest in peace!

I would like to end with a poem by Christian D. Larson (ChristianLarson.wwwhubs.com), entitled "Dream On".

Dream on, fair soul, dream on.
Thy visions are not in vain.
Other and greater worlds are waiting for thee.
Dream on, fair soul, dream on.

Let thy spirit ascend to the supreme heights
of those greater worlds where thou shall behold
the glory and splendor of that sublime existence
that is in store for thee.

And let nothing that may come or go in thy waking hours cause thee to forget what thou hast seen.

For the time is near when the dreams of the night shall rise with the morning, but shall not depart with the setting sun.

What thou hast seen in thy visions shall come to remain; and what thy lofty moments have revealed to thee shall become thine own forever.

The Man Who Did Not Listen

This story is about a man who did not listen. It happened on an island called Montserrat, West Indies, in a hospital where I was a patient. Montserrat is called the Emerald Isle of the West because it is very beautiful. The soil is very rich, maybe due to the volcano that is still active. The island is blessed with lovely beaches and a variety of fish, animals, fruits, and birds. Many hills and mountains of the island enhance its beauty. There is very little crime, and murders are rare since the people are peace-loving and friendly.

My story is about a man who suffered from diarrhea. His doctor prescribed dark toasted white bread, and black tea, as a remedy, and told the man not to eat anything else. The diet was a challenge for the man, but he was improving, not making the usual number of trips to the bathroom, and doing fine.

But did the sick man have a strong will power? Would he sacrifice his will power for his desires, looking at and smelling the food his fellow patients were eating? Did it affect him? Did he have an urge for food and was he getting hungry? Was there a battle raging within, between his will power and desires? He was improving, and I hoped for his recovery. It looked as if he were listening to the doctor.

I did not know that he was a member of the

17

Pentecostal Church nor what role his beliefs played in his life. Later on, fellow church members will play a big role in his life. The members of the Pentecostal Church are called brothers and sisters. I don't know what he told them about the diarrhea or if they were aware of how sick he was. On many occasions, we assume when we have relatives in the hospital that the food is so bland that they need something to cheer them up. On that special Sunday, the relatives, brothers and sisters in the Lord, visited him. They brought dishes of deliciously cooked food hoping to cheer him up.

Choices determine our future. The brother had a choice: he could continue to use the ever-present will power to resist, or he could give in to his desire for the food brought to him. Maybe the brother was tantalized by the appealing cooked food, or maybe he was encouraged to taste the food and was told, "It won't harm you this time!"

The man who would not listen could not resist the food. He chose desire over will power. He ate the food, and soon his visits to the bathroom accelerated. He died a few days later.

Only when you listen with your heart will you be able to hear.

INSIGHTS

Contentment

Forget not, O man or woman, that your present station on earth is appointed by the wisdom of the Eternal.

Who knows the heart?

Who sees the vanity of all thy wishes?

Who, often in mercy, denies your request?

Yet for all reasonable, honest endeavors, his benevolence hath established a probability of success in the nature of things.

The discomfort you feel; the misfortunes you experience, behold the root from which they spring, even thy own folly, thy own pride, thy own distempered fancy.

Grumble not, therefore, at the dispensation of God, but correct thine own heart. Neither imagine in your mind, "If I had wealth, or power or leisure, I should be happy." For know that they all bring to their several possessors their peculiar inconveniences.

The poor man sees not the vexations and anxieties of the rich. He experiences not the difficulties and perplexities of power. Neither does he know the wearisome leisure and therefore the feeling of dejection or discontent.

But envy not the appearance of happiness

20

in any man for he knows not the secret of grief.

To be satisfied with little is the greatest wisdom. He that increases his riches increases his cares, but a contented mind is a hidden treasure, and trouble finds it not.

Goodness is the race, which God hath set him to run, and happiness is the goal none can arrive at until he hath finished his course and received his crown in the mansions of eternity.

Unto Thee I Grant...

No Time To Quit

There comes a time in everyone's life when they want to call it quits, to just give up because of the burdens placed on life.

Do we ever think about our heart that never ceases working? It faces challenges from you, and me, but ignores the interruptions and continues working. Why does the heart work so diligently and unselfishly? What is the reason?

Maybe the reason is that the heart is very special. This organ circulates the blood that keeps us healthy. Our heart is also the source of love, and because of that love, it nourishes all of the organs in the body. It shows no favoritism. It treats all the organs the same.

We all love our hearts. Sometimes we listen to its movement. Our heart beats and we are very fascinated, mystified.

Yes, I say thanks to my heart for without its vibrations and example, where would I be? I will never think about quitting when faced with life's challenges.

Point Of View

From an intellectual point of view, I am in agreement with your hypotheses about the conditions in the world.

If, as humans, we could glimpse into hidden worlds, what a difference it would make in the way we think!

I have an opinion:

I am a spark emanating from the Divine Flame, and my mission on Mother Earth is to know myself.

What we need are thinkers, not reactionaries.

Shadows

Hypothetically, suppose what we are taught in the great school of Life is false.

And what we call Reality is but shadows!

The Hands

If I could talk to my hands, I would be awed by the stories they would tell.

I wondered how many instances or times I am conscious of my hands!

Even as a baby, a bottle with food was put into my hands. When I started to crawl, was I aware of my hands? As my hands grew and became stronger, I realized how important they are to the body as a member.

Without hands, life would be cumbersome, maybe frustrating! Imagine what it would be like taking a bath, brushing your teeth, getting dressed or eating without hands.

The hands are used for cooking, peeling vegetables, cutting, baking, and putting food in pots and ovens.

Hands are used for so many things that they seem magical.

The hands are used for getting dressed, undressed, getting into bed and removing the coverlet.

Hands are used in prayer, for hugging and caressing, and for doing many other interesting things.

The hands are beautifully made with the palms, fingers and nails.

Hands are used for writing, drawing, sketching and painting, holding, and operating a phone and computer.

Yes, the hands are awesome!

When the God of our hearts decided to create man, He said to Himself/Herself, man should be independent and would need tools, different tools, so he designed man with hands. It so happens that the hands become very important and handy later.

As the story goes, Adam and Eve goofed. The serpent outsmarted Eve, our first Mother. Adam knew what Eve did, but our first father, Adam, did not have the courage to be responsible. When the test or challenge came, he blamed Eve. Adam deceived himself, and both of them were sent forth from the garden.

They were given the responsibility to till the ground from whence they were taken.

The tool?

The hands.

The Lady, Dogs, Cat And Ducks

The day is cloudy. The sunlight, as usual, is always trying to be. Colors of the clouds are whitish on a background of what seem to be white and blue. The sunlight on the leaves of the trees seems like glittering gold. Yes, there are trees and houses all around, and yet I see many ducks very often. In my community, it rains frequently so there is always an ample supply of water.

I am fascinated by ducks and how they relate with each other. Most of the time, I see two ducks, and sometimes many of them get together, as if they were having a meeting. The meeting is usually by a waterhole where rain has collected.

There is a mixture of single dwellings, condos and townhouses where I live. In the area, there is an abundance of trees, plants, and grassy spaces filled with all sorts of animals and insects, such as, dogs, cats, ducks, lizards, ants, snakes and squirrels.

It is one of my neighbors walking her dogs that fascinate me the most. The cat seems to be always on its own. I do not know its gender, but it acts like a great hunter. It behaves as if it owns this section of the complex. Yes, it is a black cat, and he, the ducks, the dogs and the lady seem to be great friends.

My neighbor, who walks her dogs, also feeds the cat. So he discreetly hangs around as part of the family.

She also feeds the ducks. In the morning when the dogs are taken for a walk, the cat walks at a distance behind the dogs, and even the ducks join the parade sometimes. It is fascinating and beautiful to see this parade. The lady, two dogs, a cat and sometime the ducks all go for a walk. What a sight!

I wonder how many neighbors see what I see. Does it really matter?

I enjoy it. Who Cares!

The Lizard

I moved the plywood and there was a lizard. My attention was on the weeds that were growing among the grass in the lawn. My intention was to eradicate as many as possible with the weed killer.

Impulsively, I sprayed the lizard many times as it ran under the eve of the roof. When I looked up, I saw it was stunned, lying there helplessly. Instantly, I felt pity, compassion, and pain for the lizard, sensing its stress, pain, and possible death.

I looked up again at the lizard. There was no place for it to hide, so there was nothing the lizard could do but stare at me. As we stared at each other, I saw no fear in his eyes. He had accepted his fate. I suppose it was wondering what it had done to me to be treated thus. I looked up again, and the lizard was no longer there. I imagine it had fallen or maybe died.

As I reflected on my actions, I asked myself why I had maimed or killed an innocent lizard.

The Power Within

But there is more to it than this.

If on a higher level we plan our ordeals and trials, it follows that there must also be implanted in the soul the power necessary to overcome them. This is axiomatic; to recognize it is most essential.

Our suffering and trials are not meaningless blows of chance, but a destiny planned and directed by our higher selves for our essential character evolution. As we face each trial on our allegorical journey through the dark forest and the perilous sea, we receive the strength to overcome by tapping into springs of Eternal Power.

The power may not be apparent until facing the ordeal. Our conscious mind is unaware of it, but if we can rejoice with joy and affirmation in the face of our trials, the power will be forthcoming, as if by magic. This is cooperation with a higher world. It is a technique of heroic action.

If we do not grasp the deeper meaning of the soul's trials and tribulations, we may indeed fall into despair and imagine that all is meaningless hardship: "a tale told by an idiot, full of sound and fury, signifying nothing," as Macbeth found after his failure.

To say that the strength to overcome is implanted in us does not mean that everyone will overcome.

There are many who fail on the quest – heroes who are vanquished, weaklings who are daunted by the perils they face.

He who achieves is indeed a hero. He learns to say "yes" courageously to the opportunities offered where before he might have timidly held back. It is a path of valor and joy, adventure and exploration into the unknown. Every myth, every fairy tale, most great dramas, and all epic poetry focus on the symbol of a hero. The myths speak to us in symbolic form of timeless truths intensely relevant to our life – far more so than any of the academic philosophies that we study.

The Snake And The Rat

The day is sunny and bright. Butterflies are flying near now and then. The sky is blue with scattered white clouds.

I am reminded of a story recently told to me by a friend. She loves all sorts of animals such as cats, dogs, birds, snakes, and others. Many of them share her abode.

I was told that snakes will not eat dead animals. The other day she brought a rat for the snake's dinner. Normally, the snake would pounce on the rat and eat it. However, this rat survived in the cage with the snake for a few weeks.

So the rat said to itself, "I will not be eaten by this snake. I will make a plan. I will befriend the snake. I will create an environment of fear by harassing the snake and beating it up now and then. In the meantime, I will plan my escape."

The plan seemed to work because my friend saw the rat smacking the snake!

One day, she took the cage to clean it outside in her backyard, which is a natural habitat for wild animals, and the plan of escape happened. Maybe the door of the cage wasn't closed properly, and somehow the snake and the rat seized the opportunity and escaped back to where they belong, even if for a short time, back to nature.

I just saw a tiny leaf falling to the ground. What a privilege.

Without A Plan

Imagine beginning life's journey without a map. It is like a log floating on the ocean without a rudder to steer you into the unknown. You are at the mercy of the current and the wind because from the start of the journey you consciously put yourself in the hands of chance. Imagine the chaos and loneliness that lie ahead.

Questions rise. Why was there no plan? Did you communicate with your parents or friends? What happened?

Whatever is happening is very prevalent; most people do not think for themselves. They are lazy, and this is one reason that there are so many chaotic lives. In an unsettled life, nothing seems to be normal and everything seems to be out of place. You imagine something is occurring in your life of which you are unaware.

From the beginning of your journey, because of your duality, there were always two voices speaking, and you had to choose one of them.

You decided to do it your way! You made that choice because it was the decision you had to make. In your journey, many unfinished things were left behind. Although you were reminded, you ignored it, all because you had no plan.

As you continued on your journey, you felt

disturbed, unhappy, and wondered what went wrong. You either forgot or were not aware of the Law Of Karma, also known as cause and effect, action and reaction, reaping what you sow.

You felt hopeless and overpowered, at that moment when everything seemed darkest with no way out. The voice you had ignored spoke and told you everything was just fine.

The voice continued, "Because you do not know who you are, you have ignored me all these years and suffered through the ignorance of not knowing."

You are the handicap you must face; you are the one who must choose your place. You must say where you want to go, and how much you are willing to study the truth to know.

God equips you for life, but he lets you decide what you want to be in that life.

INSPIRATION

A Story

My window faces the east, so on a sunny day my room is brilliantly lit. This morning was no exception. As I looked out of the window, I found myself in a dream-like state, thinking and adoring the creative work of the Absolute. It was awesome!

As I continued to gaze, I saw a bird that landed on a telephone wire, stayed awhile, and then flew away. Suddenly the birds seemed to be flying in all directions. They were enjoying themselves. I heard some of the birds singing beautiful, melodious songs. Listen and sometime, the melodies may relax you.

I noticed the clouds were changing, creating new sceneries and all the colors man can imagine were there. Mother Nature (God) gives the minerals, vegetation, animals, and men everything he needs freely. So the question must be asked: Why are humans starving and lacking clean water?

I love nature and the outdoors. I don't visit the beaches as I once did. Now I spend more time with the trees, flowers, butterflies and bees. I like to dig in the soil and look at the worms, bugs, ants, and the many other insects. You may be surprised if I say we are all related.

I watched in amazement as the clouds tried to block the sunlight. As I looked, I did not see when the clouds gave way to the sunlight. The sun and the clouds seem to play a game often, like hide and seek. We humans know that the sun is life; without its energy, vibrations, and rays, everything would die.

We also heard of a man who was called the son of God who preached love and said that we can have eternal life, if we believe with all our hearts. I love God and nature and look forward with expectation both mornings and evenings to the physical world for the displays of the various art sceneries that can be seen whenever the clouds are not blocking the sun.

An Ordeal

I am looking at a scene that I see almost every morning: the plants, trees, grass, houses, and the landscapes that Mother Nature creates. My window faces the East, and it is through that window that I have the pleasure to appreciate different scenes. At this moment, the sun seems to be clearing a path through the clouds as if to exhibit its colors, from a mystical rich golden yellow to a bright silvery color. If there was no sun, what would happen to the planet? Minus the sun, air, fire, and water, there would be no life. As I ponder my life and imagine how privileged I am, I thank that creative source.

This time last year I made a decision that would change my life forever – a choice that was apparent -- stay or leave home. I chose the latter; that was bold and daring. I entered the world of the unknown. It was a strange new world that I chose. I had other responsibilities that seemed to exaggerate my dilemma. I knew deep down inside that I had to be strong or I would not survive.

Each day seemed as if my world was not real, but I was striving to overcome and knew I would be fine. I was looking for a place to live, but I was determined not to live in a house where I would be uncomfortable. Many of the places that were shown to me in my thoughts seemed deplorable. The people who were living in those dwelling places seem contented.

The strange thing about my ordeal was that although I had family and friends, I never confided in them, maybe because I was in my dream world most of the time. I finally found an apartment I liked and moved there; it did not lessen my loneliness. In the mornings I would walk, but never participated in the physical and social activities that took place there. Strange as it may sound, my peace of mind came from a picture of my granddaughter. In my imagination, I knew and felt her spirit. She was always looking at me, assuring me, everything was fine and not to worry.

In retrospect, my adventure was necessary; the chaos, pain and loneliness were only lessons. I needed the experiences to correct the way I was thinking. First I forgave myself, recognized the cause and forgave it; then I looked deeply into my soul. There I found all the peace, love, and health that were missing in my life. At this moment, the spirit of love and understanding dwells in the home.

Curious

I had an urge to open a book that I was looking at.

After opening the book, I looked at the page. Subjectively everything, I read, originates in the mind, even diseases we thought we would never experience.

Then my curiosity led me to another book. I opened the second book and thought what I saw was a very profound message.

The one who knows, it said, doesn't grieve over loss, because the only thing that can be lost is the unreal.

Lose everything, and the real still remains. In the middle of all devastation and disease, hidden treasures are buried. Whenever you look at rubble, look closely. Remember, whatever we hold on to is already dead because it is in the past. We die every moment and will eventually discover the gate to unending life.

My Soul

Unconsciously, I have known you from (creation) birth, but our relationship was not as exciting as now. We are so close now that I can hear your voice speaking to me and feel your presence. When I hear your voice and listen, everything works harmoniously. When I ignore that voice, in any moment, whatever is happening is in disarray. Sometimes, I know that I should do a chore, yet put it off and it seems to multiply. Stress and impatience seem to enter thoughts and aggravate my emotions.

I am happy that now I am aware of your importance and how vital it is for me to listen to your voice. I know my thoughts and attitude will make the difference of how I evolve. I also know, without your presence, I wouldn't be alive. I know I am your reflection. You are pure and undefiled, pristine. Because of my ignorance, I took you for granted all these years. Now I am aware of your presence, and there is nothing I can do to get rid of you.

All I can do is surrender and let go so that I will be helped on my mystical journey. As I travel the mystical path, I know that it will not be easy. There are so many distractions on that path that Will and Choice are very important. Some choices I make will be detrimental. I will need super energy to resist the attractions of the material world, which only you, the soul, can supply.

When my thinking, attitude, and actions are positive and harmonized with the pure spiritual character of my soul, and are all encompassing, I know that even though I am an individual, we humans are One because Divine energy flows through all things.

I am happy that now, I am always thinking of you (My Soul).

Provoking Thoughts

Some of you may not understand what I am saying and some will. Jesus said, "Some people will hear, and some will not hear, and some will see, and some will not see."

What was he talking about? Was it the senses? What do you think?

At this moment, I am in the mood to write and I want to share my thoughts. Maybe someone will read my words. I am hoping they are beneficial.

I am going to share what I imagine on communication. The lack of communication creates confusion, mistrust within one self and without.

Life is intangible – man plays games he does not understand. Later on, as he progresses in life, he experiences adverse emotions that are perplexing and he wonders why! Life is a process always in motion creating cause and effect, sowing and reaping.

Only the wise man that dwells within will be able to see and hear the impact and soften the effects of his creation. Man should always examine his thoughts; those thoughts are what become the impetus that builds our character, helps us becoming loving and useful citizens, and helps build a world of peace and happiness starting with ourselves.

As some would say, communicating thoughts

of love, not taking anything personally, not assuming anything, and always trying to do our best can help build a better world. Mentally, man creates his own world, so why not build a world of peace?

Emotional battles are fought within before they become manifest and produce mistrust, hate, and greed.

Imagine a world where there is no fear, a world where we will reflect each other's love. Can humanity tap into this force or vibratory energy to create such a state of consciousness?

What are your thoughts?

Reflections
(The White Spot)

I looked down and saw a spot on the floor. I wondered how it got there. Not paying attention, I started to clean what I imagined was a spot on the floor.

I scrubbed and scrubbed, but the spot did not budge. Suddenly, as if by magic, my left hand moved toward the spot, and I noticed that the spot was nowhere to be found.

Believe it or not, it was only a reflection I saw on the floor. The sunlight had streamed through the white curtain and reflected its color.

I wondered how many times I have been fooled by a reflection. Sometimes I have seen myself reflected in others and did not have a clue. Sometimes I blamed others when it was only me.

The elusive spot on the floor is a lesson to me, of how many times I have been fooled by not paying attention to myself and where I am.

So I say, "Thank you, invisible spot, for the lesson you have taught me."

UNITY, Or

This moment the sky is cloudy. Looking at the area that appears as the edge of the sky seems dark. The other places in the sky seem bright, although the sun is hiding behind clouds.

A few days ago, I was asked to lend my thoughts on Unity, which seemed very interesting indeed. As I look at the TV and listen to the radio, I heard dismal news of the failures of the financial institutions at home and worldwide. The word, 'unity,' became even more important. So I asked myself, "What is unity? Is it an entity? Where does unity reside? Is unity a virtue?"

I am told that unity is strength and that without unity we become fragmented and fall apart. The question is: "Where can unity be found?"

My opinion is that unity cannot be found outside of one's spiritual self (The I AM). All good that emanates from that source is love, health, harmony and peace of mind. Our thoughts can be harmonious, which is serenity and unity, or disharmony, which results in disorder, pain, disease, and death. My thoughts are things. I am consciousness and feeling. Whatever my thoughts are, that is what I am at that moment.

Thoughts, like electricity, can manifest positively in various forms such as engines, light bulbs, elevators, but also negatively in destructive ways. This is a good analogy for us humans. When I am satisfied within, then everything will be unity.

Christ's message to us is that he cannot do anything except through the Father. Who is the Father? Also, he said that I can do greater things than he. What did he mean by that?

It has been raining all day, off and on; the wind seems to be kind to the trees. The branches and leaves seem to be at peace, and unity was displayed in Mother Nature.

When I cultivate unity in my subjective thought world, I am one with all things!

You Can Be Molded In His Image

According to Romans 8:29, "For whom he did fore know, he also did predestinate to be conformed to the image of his Son, that he might be the first born among many brethrens."

Your goal as a Christian is to become Christ-like.

The *Bible* says you are an ambassador of Christ and that he personally makes his appeal to the world through you.

The only way you can properly represent Jesus to the world is to let his character show through in your attitudes and actions.

This can only happen through Divine transformation, and that is exactly what God had in mind from the beginning of time.

God predestined you to be molded into his image and share inwardly his likeness.

He said, "Behold, as the clay is in the potter's hand, so are ye in mine hand...." Jeremiah 18:6.

In your relationship with God, you are the clay and He the potter, and you must never forget that. Become pliable in the Master Potter's hands as He molds you into a vessel He can use to change many lives.

Ending your day right!

50

LOVE

Eloise

Eloise, I love you.

May our life together be God-like.

May it be blissful.

May it be carefree.

May it be child-like.

May it be innocent.

May our love float

and be part of whatever it encounters.

May our love be God-love.

Eloise, I love you.

My Plans

My plans were that after retirement I would return to my native home, Montserrat.

My plan was to go to the beach as often as I could. My plan was to enjoy the sea and the sun. My plan was to build a boat.

My plan was to have a garden. My plan was to enjoy the food I planted and share the produce with others.

My plan was to enjoy the landscape.

My plan was to enjoy our native foods.

My plan was to live with life and nature.

But my plans were all shattered when I met a beautiful, brown-eyed woman who is now my wife. And I live in Fort Lauderdale.

My Valentine

Eloise is my brown-eyed wife of many dreams.

We shared so many things together -- blissful moments, sad moments – but we knew they were life's lessons.

We taught each other so many things, and always hoped the best for each other.

We love each other and hope that one day we will have peace of mind.

May our love continue to grow as a fruit-bearing tree so that we may enjoy the fruits of our love.

May love, health, and the precious gift of peace of mind be ours.

Happy Valentine's Day from your friend, lover and husband.

My Wife Always Calls

My wife, who has to work, always calls home to make sure I am all right. She calls many times to find out what I am doing.

She always calls to find out how my time is spent. She wants me to read, play the piano, or do something constructive.

She always calls home to let me know what she is doing. She always calls to let me know if she will be late coming home.

My wife loves me, and I love my wife.

When she's leaving work,

My wife always calls.

Personal And Spiritual Love

Love ye one another. A beautiful saying this, for it is an appeal to the very core of our nature, which is the Divine within us, the inner god whose essence is celestial splendor. The essential Light of us is almighty Love.

Love is the great attractive power that links thing-to-thing and human heart to human heart.

The higher one goes in evolution, the closer love enwraps its tendrils through the entire fiber of one's being and the more the human heart expands with love until finally it embraces in its folds the entire Universe. Thus, we come to love all things both great and small without distinction of place or time.

Oh, the blessedness of this feeling, of this realization, for impersonal (spiritual) love is Divine. Personal (physical) love is a reflection of this spiritual love, but personal love is fallible because the energy is so feeble. Anything that has as its motivating cause the desire for personal benefit is not true love. If the mind and heart fill solely with personal love, then this love becomes fragmented. For example, deciding that I love this, but not that, or that this is mine. Emotionally, there is always a war within for dominance; the result is always restlessness and insecurity, and that breeds mistrust.

Impersonal love is beautiful and has no trace of the things we dislike. It is always kind to everything and to everybody – to beings and things both great and small. It is intuitive, responsible, trusting, confident, and compassionate. These aspects indeed bring happiness, strength, and joy. Cultivate them. But we will not fully understand these grand qualities nor truly feel them if our head is filled with personal limited feelings and thoughts.

Kahlil Gibran expresses these grand qualities in his book, *The Prophet*.

"Love has no other desire but to fulfil itself.

"But if you love and must needs have desires, let these be your desires:

"To melt and be like a running brook that sings its melody to the night.

"To know the pain of too much tenderness.

"To be wounded by your own understanding of love;

And to bleed willing and joyfully.

"To wake at dawn with a winged heart and give thanks for another day of loving;

"To rest at the noon hour and meditate love's ecstasy;

"To return home at eventide with gratitude;

And then to sleep with a prayer for the beloved in your heart and a song of praise upon your lips."

Let me end my story about love by saying, "Only those who contact the source of true love and cultivate this love will experience peace and happiness."

As you read my story, I hope you can find this feeling in your heart.

Thoughts On Love

The question is: What is love?

It is evident, in my mind, every conscious moment of our waking hours of our human life; this question is asked over and over throughout the world. So, what is love? I was told that I live in the Divine Creator, the source of all manifestation. It is mentioned in the *Bible*, "For in him we live, and move, and have our being..." Very interesting. I will say that I am Divine; all of us are. We are the microcosm of the macrocosm; we all have the attributes of the creator.

Love is a virtue of the creator; love is my consciousness in you and everywhere.

Love is beauty and attraction. It cements everything.

It knows no evil, only peace, bliss, and health; it is ever eternal.

Ignorance will interfere and seem to dim the brilliance of the light of love, but love will always be there. The clouds are trying to overshadow the light of the sun, but the sun will always be there.

There are many aspects of love. Humans fragmented love, and we have many meanings for love.

The love I am writing about is very patient. Although it permeates our being, we will never find it unless we seek it, nourish it, and share it. Yes, we have to know

59

it, feel it, and surrender to it so that it can mold us into what we should be.

Love has a tool that is called reason. If humans learn to reason with one another, we will come to a better understanding of who we are.

Love is a mystery to the majority of humanity, but there is a small group of humans who know what love is.

In our physical world, the rose is a symbol of love, but no matter how beautiful the rose, it has thorns. So to admire and love a rose, you don't pick it, and you don't destroy it. You leave it on the rose bush; you admire, love and nurture it. You let it be free because love cannot be imprisoned. It has to be free.

Yes, there is love. What do you think?

NATURE

Borders

How lovely it is to cross a boundary.

The traveling man becomes a primitive man in many ways the same as a Nomad.

I love everything at home, but I have to leave it. Tomorrow I will love other homes, places and buildings. I won't leave my heart behind me as they say in love letters. I am going to carry it with me on my journey because I need it, always.

I am a nomad not a farmer. I am an admirer of the unfaithful, the changing and the fantastic. I don't care to attach my love to one bare place on this earth. I believe that love is only a symbol. It is when love becomes too attached to one thing, one faith, or one virtue that I become very attentive.

Good luck to the farmer! Good luck to the man who owns the place, the man who works it, the faithful, virtuous! I can love him; I can revere him; I can envy him. But I have wasted half of my life trying to live his.

I wanted to be something that I am not. I even wanted to be a poet and a middle-class person at the same time. I wanted to be an artist and a man of fantasy, but I also wanted to be a good man, a man at home.

This all went on for a long time, until I knew that a symbol cannot be both, that I am a nomad, a man who searches and not a man who keeps. A long time I suffered myself before gods and laws that were idols for me. That was what I did wrong. This was my anguish, my complicity in the world of pain.

I increased the world's guilt and anguish by doing violence to myself, by not daring to walk to my own salvation. The way to salvation leads neither to the left or right: it leads into your own heart. There alone is God, and there alone is peace.

But the longing to get on the other side of everything already settled, makes me, and everyone like me, a road sign to the future. If there were many more people like me who loathed the borders between countries, then there would be no more wars and blockades.

Nothing on earth is more disgusting, more contemptible, than borders. They are like cannons and generals. As long as peace, loving kindness, and tolerance reign, nobody pays any attention to them. But as soon as war and insanity appear, they become urgent and sacred.

Landscape

Mother Nature displays her landscapes every moment in pictures, even if clouds and rain often veil them.

They are always in motion; they keep coming and going, changing and becoming.

Many times, early in the mornings, I tried to capture the change of colors from the golden sun to the silvery clouds with no success.

Why all the mystery? Is Nature trying to tell us that there is something hidden behind the appearances we are seeing?

Nature puts on a show, every moment of every day, and no finite being will ever be able to make an exact copy.

The displays are mysterious, awesome and beautiful. We humans can describe them as we see them.

Mankind can try to use its God-given intelligence to copy what its emotional eyes see and sometimes even falsely to take credit for one of God's creations.

On The Sunny Beach

The day was hot and sunny. On the sea, silvery colors reflected from the sun on the water. The waves on the ocean seemed moderate, and the vibratory force or energy seemed normal.

The water was clear and warm, and one had a feeling that the ocean was inviting all the visitors to enter its abode. It was saying subtly, "Come into me; I love you and will make you feel happy for the moment." The beach was not crowded then, and the people were doing what people do when they go to the beach to have fun.

There has to be a magical attraction that draws so many people to the ocean and beaches. The beaches seem to offer a sense of freedom that is comfortable. Families can have fun together. Ladies can dress sexy and not feel remorseful. Everyone who wants a tan can have one.

There are many things the family can do such as building sand castles, walking the beach, and swimming in the ocean. Children can dig holes in the sand and play games with the water. The water usually wins the game because the child typically digs a hole just beyond where he or she thinks the water will reach, but the water gets there and causes the child a lot of work. The fun begins because they think they can bale the water out of the hole before the next wave comes in and fills up the hole again.

On the beach, there are many exciting things to watch. Some grown-ups would go into the ocean, splash around, dive, and even become very acrobatic – having fun with the sea and sometimes experiencing that peace we all love.

As with everything else in life, a plan is needed even for going to the beach. Many items are necessary such as water to drink and snacks to eat.

Many lovers go to the beach to have fun. They get into the water and then hug, kiss, and embrace one another. They seem relaxed and peaceful; unbeknownst to them, they are sharing their feelings and love with the ocean.

The sea and the beach are both rich in minerals. Our bodies absorb the electromagnetic current from the sea and the sand. It is no wonder that we are subconsciously drawn to the ocean.

I grew up near the beach, and the ocean and the waves always fascinated me. Sometimes the waves seem very angry, especially when the wind becomes irate, forcing the waves to act like bullies. At other times when the wind is calm and the under current, like the riptides, are in harmony, everything seems to be at peace.

When we look at the ocean as waves are acting uncontrollably, we know that it is only for a while because everything changes and becomes something else.

As a matter of fact, the ocean and the waves are the same element (water). Like the ocean, we humans fight with ourselves all the time because we do not know who we are, and wrong thoughts can create disharmony.

On this day, the temperature was rising, but the sea breeze had me feeling just fine, swimming and enjoying all that Mother Nature gives so freely. On the beach the sea is calm, and the waves are breaking effortlessly. All one has to do is to watch the children playing, the birds soaring, and endless sky to become one with the moment – on the beach.

Rain Drops

It was a sunny day. Then it became cloudy; suddenly a few raindrops began falling everywhere.

Drops in the pool were a beautiful sight to see. As the raindrops fell lazily into the pool, they seemed so scattered, so slow, and looked as if they could be counted. The wind was busy pushing the raindrops. They looked pressured as they tried to resist the force of the wind. Then they stopped resisting and were falling in a slanted formation.

Raindrops became energized falling faster. Those falling in the pool created a picture as if the water was boiling; all that was seen was countless bubbles as if merging, becoming one. As the rain fell, the sound of thunder was heard as if far away. As one listened, melodious sounds were heard. The raindrops were creating enchanting music; nearby birds were singing.

The roar of the thundering was still heard; the raindrops were slowing down; birds were still singing, and the trees, grass and others were grateful for the raindrops.

The sun was shining brightly again, and the dark clouds disappeared. But raindrops began falling again. It was a beautiful sight to see the shower through the glow of the sunlight.

JOY COMETH IN THE MORNING

Soon the sun will set and display many colors before disappearing on the horizon. It is quiet and peaceful as the shadows creep across the skies.

Sexuality

Your identity is simple; it is not dependent on your psychological or biological sexuality.

Your sexual characteristics represent only one portion of your person. They provide vital areas of expression and focal points about which to group experience. Your sexual qualities are a part of your nature, but they do not define it.

Your beliefs structure your experience both individually and en masse. Evidential material, contrary to those ideas, shows itself but seldom, or in distorted or exaggerated form.

It is quite natural, biologically and psychologically, to operate in certain fashions that are not acceptable to your society and that seem to run counter to your picture of mankind's history.

The Avocado Tree

It is a beautiful spring morning. The sun is beaming down on the avocado tree and a beautiful lawn. The grass is freshly cut. What a sight! The sun glistens on the beautifully designed leaves that stand motionless as if there was no wind.

There is something pristine about the scene. I feel its serenity and peace. It is a moment of pure joy.

The avocado tree is shedding old leaves, and new ones are replacing them. The process has been in progress for some time. Why is the tree ridding itself of the old leaves? If the tree kept the old leaves, would it affect its growth?

The spring equinox is here: the season of new life and growth, a time of awesome energy that affects all living things. What would have happened to the tree if it had kept its old leaves?

The avocado tree seems happy with its colorful leaves – some green, others with tints of red, and the blossoms with hues of yellow. What would have happened if the tree had not let go of its old leaves?

The Birds

I am listening to the sound of the birds – different sounds -- some soft, some loud.

The sky is blue with scattered white shapes on the blue background! The day is sunny with the sunlight glistening on the trees and leaves.

As I admire the awesome beauty of Mother Nature, I observe the competition of the trees for sunlight. The trees that get the sunlight will survive. The battle for sunlight is so fierce that those trees that have the capacity actually grow taller, overshadowing those trees or plants that cannot compete in their plant world.

The plant battle for sunlight in the plant world is mirrored daily in our human lives.

Can we humans do something about it?

I say YES!

RELATIONSHIPS

A Woman

It takes a special man to understand a woman.

Sometimes she behaves like her counterpart, Eve, the first woman.

Sometimes she is blamed for the choice she makes.

Sometimes her mood changes suddenly.

Sometimes she is restless.

Sometimes she doesn't know what is wrong with her.

Sometimes she doesn't know what to wear.

Sometimes she doesn't' know what to eat.

Sometimes she is happy, sometimes sad.

Sometimes she is mischievous.

Sometimes she is just fun.

Sometimes she is loving and kind.

Sometimes she wants to be held closely; sometimes she wants to be left alone.

Sometimes she has it all together and knows how to do everything.

Sometimes she doesn't know how to style her hair; she just messes it up.

Sometimes she doesn't know what color her fingernails should be painted.

Sometimes she knows that she is creative.

Sometimes she knows that she is a powerhouse.

Sometimes she knows that without her there would be no existence; the world would die slowly.

Sometimes she knows that without her, what would men do?

It takes a special man to understand a woman.

Females

The morning after the art class session, I reflected on what I saw. A student and I were late and when I entered the classroom, everyone was sitting as if assigned to a group. There was a lot of chattering. "Why all the talking?" I wondered.

The majority of the class is female; only the teacher and I are males.

At the moment of entry, I noticed the teacher talking to a female, not realizing that she was one of us. In the meantime, the females were having a ball chatting. I was amazed by their empathy and sincerity for each other; all of them seemed as if they were having fun.

Upon entering the classroom, I was greeted and felt welcome and wanted.

In the meantime, the teacher--a gentle soul, was helping a student (who had been absent for a while) catch up with those working on the same project.

The females continued to talk and have fun, unconsciously exchanging beautiful thoughts and words with each other, which in reality are really stories.

As a spectator, I was amused, perplexed and found the scene interesting. The female group is made up of many life styles and beliefs and yet shared a common bond.

Some will say maybe because we are human, but I imagine it is something more.

The teacher finished helping the student update her work. He apologized to us for the delay and began his tutoring.

Yes, we all want to be great artists. To walk a mile we all begin with a single step. So cultivate patience, and be courageous on your journey to become an artist.

Thank God for females! Without them, what would we males do?

I See Your Movement; I Hear Your Words

I see your movement; I hear your words. Your words and movement are yours. Why not share your movement and words in a charitable fashion so that others will benefit instead of in a controlling, negative manner?

I see your movement; I hear your words. Your behavior is erratic; your sight is clouded. You are lost and don't know where to go.

I see your movement; I hear your words. You are in your created world. Those of us who love you are hoping you will tap into the all-healing force called Love. In your imaginary world, we are your subjects, to be controlled at will.

I see your movement; I hear your words. When the Higher Self, Soul, Mind is neglected, life seems meaningless.

Intuitively, there is no spiritual guidance. You begin to feel that no one loves you. You begin to feel restless, abandoned, and begin to fantasize. Nothing seems to be in order. Everything seems fragmented.

I see your movement; I hear your words. Frustration, stress, emotional imbalance becomes a reality. The body feels the pressure and begins to break down.

I see your movement; I hear your words. The heartaches and disease can be avoided if we change our movement and words. Go within and consult your Higher Self. There you will find love for yourself, and plenty to share.

I see your movement; I hear your words.

Interaction

Just when I think I have the answer to a problem it either disappears or becomes something else. I keep fooling myself, thinking I know, and that I'm smart, not realizing there is an invisible world where everything originates!

I must remain open and receptive to that inner Voice and remember, I'm only reflecting what I am open to receive. That is why we are told to "Know thyself." It is important for me to discern and distinguish between the different voices within me...

The Visible and the Invisible!

Letting Go

Relationships are changeable, destructive, and confusing; the question is why? Is expectation the problem? Most relationships deal with love or material things, but without feelings and emotions, there is no experience.

Love is an emotional response to the feelings I have when I am attracted to someone or something. When I say I am in love, what I really mean is that I am attracted by the aura of that person or thing; that attraction is vibratory energy. There is a sense of excitement or exhilaration as the auras harmonize with each other.

When I encounter an object to which I am attracted, I naturally want to control, possess, and preserve it for myself so that I continue to have the sense of harmony and attraction I first felt. If I succeed in possessing it, I often find myself face to face with one of the enigmas of the principle of attraction. The attraction fades and often passes away. In some cases, it turns into repulsion. Love is not to be possessed or controlled. The feeling of love is strongest when the auras involved retain their individual identities and where there is a free association between them. This means partaking lightly of close association and leaving time for separation in regular intervals throughout the relationship. If I want to enjoy a rose for the longest time possible, I don't cut it. I let it survive on the bush. It is mine to admire and love. However, when I cut it and possess it, I shorten its life and the period of attraction.

If I really love someone, then my object should be to do everything possible to give that person the freedom to be what he/she wants to be, to do what he/she wants to do, to invite him/her in, and to offer help and companionship. If I let go casily, the chances are that I won't lose my love, that the force of attraction will sustain the love I feel.

With every negative encounter, my body loses energy, and it leaves me weak. I am striving to be a peaceful and productive human. I imagine every sane person is doing all they can to acquire that inner peace that passed all understanding. When I become reactive or hurt someone's feelings, it affects me just as much as the person I made unhappy.

Deep down in my heart, I know it is hard to be loving and kind in every moment. But, when those negatives appear, if I am in a state of awareness, I will be able to recognize what is happening and do something about it even letting it pass. Because of my consciousness and feelings, I am happy or sad sometimes, but I know if I am in control, everything will be fine.

The Journey Will Be Difficult

The Journey will be difficult, especially when you and your partner dwell in two different worlds, and when you are talking and your partner is not listening. What is heard is on the surface. This can lead to misunderstanding and conflict. Especially when the blame game takes on a life of its own, and a battle of wills begin. The strife can be devastating because it leaves both opponents weak. The body is depleted of the energy it needs.

The journey will be difficult, especially when reason enters and surveys the chaotic scene. Reason will suggest forgiveness, but will forgiveness be understood by the partners, especially when the partners did all they could to destroy each other?

The journey will be difficult, especially when we understand deep in our soul that we are all here on this earth for a purpose- to love. If we do, we will have love, trust and respect for our partners and the whole world.

Wouldn't it be a great experience of joy, peace, and satisfaction if we could say that the journey was difficult, but I got through it!

The Teacher And The Students

A middle-aged man walked into the classroom. He looked grandfatherly and friendly and walked quietly to the room that seemed to be a place for storage. After a while, he went to his desk and sat down, scrutinizing the papers lying on his desk.

Then he rose and said, "My name is so-and-so. I am your teacher, and I am going to write my name and phone number on the blackboard. You can call me at home, but won't be able to reach me until after seven p.m. I spend a lot of time at this school, and I have been teaching here for a very long time.

"As a young man, I attended many art classes at different colleges and universities. I was also a student of Pablo Picasso. When I mention my experience to my children, they think that I am joking."

He then asked the students if they had any painting experience. The response was varied. He wanted the students to get to know each other, so he asked each student to say their name, where they were from, and what they would like to paint.

He continued to speak and announced that he had clippings from news magazines that the students could choose from to copy. After each student had chosen, pictures would be separated into groups, and the chosen picture would be selected through the process of elimination. Each picture selected will be voted on and compete with each other. The picture with the most votes would be declared the winner.

The teacher then printed copies of the selected pictures in black and white and gave them to the students. He then offered to make color copies for any students who were willing to pay a dollar for the process.

The teacher gave an orientation to new students and told old students they could leave and return home if they wished. Students were advised what tools they needed so that they could become artists. They were also informed class began the following Monday.

That Monday, students came prepared with a canvas, easel, and brushes. Many students felt challenged, but were soon put at ease by the comforting words of the teacher and older students. They heard many testimonies from the older students that they had never held an artist brush in their hand, but at the end of the art class were able to leave with a beautiful painting in their hand, all because of the teacher's love and patience.

Students were shown how to lay out the picture and how to transfer it to the canvas. Then the students were taught how to sketch. After the sketch was completed, it was sprayed and ready for painting.

The journey in painting began, and although most students became frustrated and ready to give up; under the watchful eye of the teacher and with the help of the more experienced students, the new students began to progress. When a student asked the teacher for help, he always replied with an encouraging word; "You are doing fine," and "How may I help?"

At the end of the last class, there was disbelief and amazement among students who saw and painted the same picture. The question can be asked:

Why?

What Is This I Call Love?

Maybe I should ask the biologist or the physicist.

Many a time I thought I was in love, only to be disappointed. Yes, I thought I found love, only to feel it fade away.

To me it was like what I call truth. Just when I think or know the truth, it fades away.

What I thought was love was very exciting, elevating me into another dimension. Those feelings were so intense that all I could do was to surrender. Those were indescribable fleeting moments.

Sometimes what I call love can lead me into a utopian world or fairyland. There, all I have to do is imagine what I want, and it materializes.

Yes, I love those funny sensations in my body. They make me feel mischievous. I have lots of fun, forgetting the advice that was given to me long ago, that love is like a beautiful rose, but be careful of the thorns.

As I journey on life's path with many of life's experiences stored in my memory banks, I realize that love is free and cannot be shackled. Because of my fear of the unknown, I live a chaotic life instead of a life of harmony.

Imagine a world where I accept others as they are and stop living a life of expectation. In that way,

I would have a better understanding of what it is I call love.

REMINDERS TO SELF

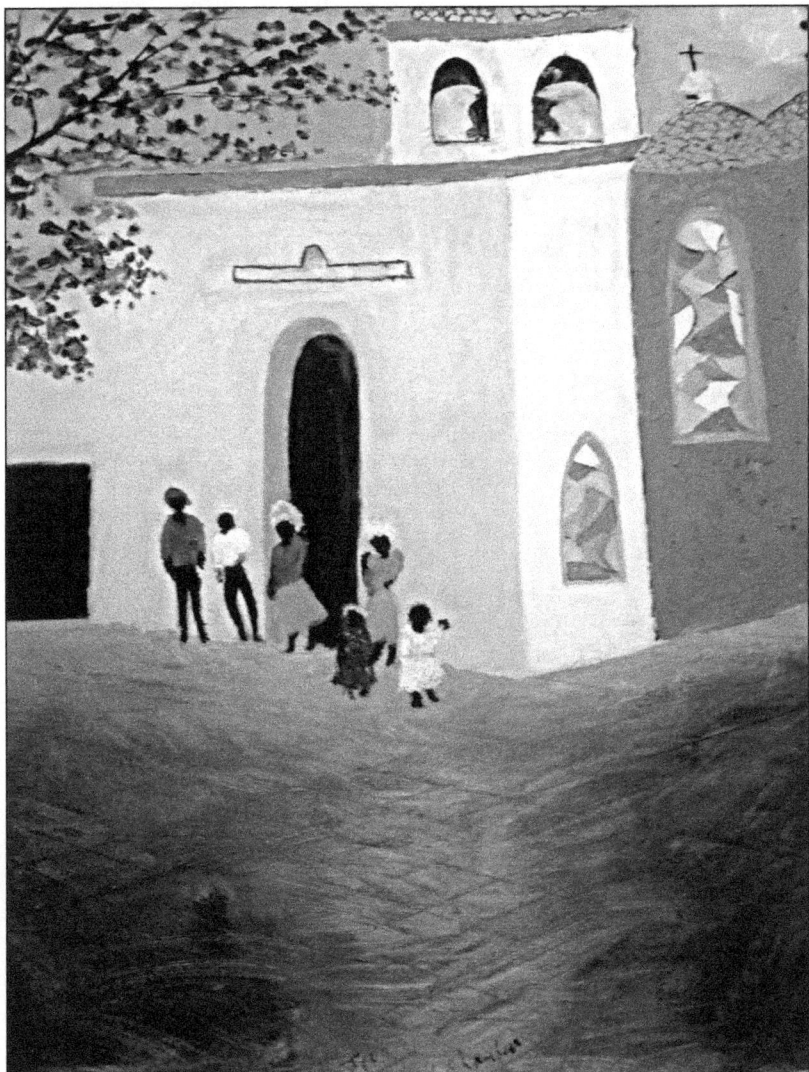

Am I Real?

Am I real?

Am I a reflection?

What am I?

I am curious.

At This Moment

What are you feeling?

Hills and Valleys

They say curiosity kills the cat!

My love of adventure led me into many hills and valleys. Most of the valleys were never comfortable. Some had a daring atmosphere, seducing, inviting and saying to my objective mind that everything is just fun.

Most of us are asleep to what is going on inside and outside of us. Until we are shocked into wakefulness, we are unaware that the valley we are in, at the moment, is deep and rocky.

In our waking state, we become retrospective and begin to ask our inner self what happened. Fear and doubt enter at that moment. I seem lost. I am in the forest of thoughts, and everything looks hopeless.

If the body-mind-sense complex is strong and experienced, I will contemplate and say I must get out of this valley. At that very moment, I start to work blindly.

As I continue, something within me begins to happen. I become more confident and know that I am helped by what we call the Master Within, the Divine Essence.

I am out of the valley again and at the top of the hill. I hope I learned a lesson to be careful of those beautiful valleys and their allurements.

Original

In the Art World, many people label things as original. In my opinion, in this finite world, nothing is original.

The question is: Where do thoughts originate?

What role do our mental faculties play?

What does the Hermetic axiom, "As above, so below. As below; so above" mean? (*The Kybalion.*)

In this world of manifestation, do we own anything?

Everything is mental.

What do you think?

Nothing is original.

Puzzle

Solve what seems a puzzle!

What?

Where?

Why?

How?

And you would be liberated!

Service

Love and serve humanity.

Praise every soul. If you cannot praise, then let him pass out of your life. Dare, dare, and then – dare more.

Do not imitate. Be original. Be inventive. Be yourself. Know yourself. Stand on your own ground. Do not lean on others. Think your own thoughts.

There is no saint without a past. There is no sinner without a future.

See God and Good in every face.

All the perfections and virtues of the Deity are hidden in you. Reveal them.

The Savior is also in you. Let His Grace emancipate you.

Some Thing

For who can fail to recognize, that when we wake in the morning, that joy, sorrow, happiness, suffering and other such experiences rise up, as if out of an unknown realm, and in a certain respect, man is given up to them?

And is there anyone who, if he reviews his whole life and soul, could deny that there must be something deeper, something at first hidden from himself, out of which his joy, suffering, happiness, grief, and all his soul experiences stream forth, and that these, no less than the external sense-perceptions, must be manifestations of an unknown world?

The Road

The road we are traveling has boulders, hills, valleys and the unseen!

As we travel this road, we (humans) are holding each other's hands.

When we let go of the others' hands, can we survive?

We all have survival tools.

Which tools will you use?

The Small Potato

Society is founded on human admiration.

We see it expressed dramatically in our lives. We cheer the winner in a prize fight and the actress for a memorable performance. We cheer our baseball or football team and shout for joy when they are the season winners.

We love a winner because we love ourselves, and, vicariously, we put ourselves in the place of the successful man; dreaming and hoping that some day it will be our turn to be cheered and applauded for outstanding achievement.

Naturally, we all have our hearts set on success. We persevere, believing that the day will come when we will reach our goal. Yet, by the very nature of things, man is a paradox. He performs various acts daily that are inconsistent with achieving importance. He persists in doing the very thing that makes him a small potato, and he takes all the time in the world to become insignificant.

All of us, more or less, receive little wounds from people in the daily struggle for contentment, and we exaggerate their significance by brooding over them. These become so great to us, though unimportant, that they make us insignificant for the time we spend coddling them, thereby wounding ourselves more in the process.

JOY COMETH IN THE MORNING

Many of us are concerned with the business of *being a small potato*. I thought it would be of value to jot down what to do and what not to do about it. With practice, you can become a small potato indeed.

DO

- *Coddle your regret.*

- *Let your mind continue to long for what has passed.*

- *Complain and be discontented when things go wrong at the time you expected the opposite.*

- *Forget that contentment should be a first step to progress.*

- *Be petty about your neighbor's good fortune.*

- *Stay hurt and disappointed about small matters.*

DON'T

- *Stop brooding over a grievance.*

- *Devote your time to worthwhile actions and feelings.*

- *Dare to think of a great thought, of wonderful affection, or lasting understanding.*

- *Remember that every scrap of time is worth saving.*

- *Remember that you are here for a few decades at best and that life is too short to be a small potato.*

Follow these precepts carefully, and I can assure you that you will become the smallest of the small potatoes.

Do nothing and remain a small potato or . . .

You

Do not condemn a single soul. When condemning others, you are condemning yourself.

Never for an instant forget that we are all *Children Of God.*

Upon the great sea of spirit, there is room for every sail.

In the limitless sky of truth, there is room for every wing.

ABOUT THE AUTHOR

James Cools Chambers was born on May 14, 1930, in Roseau, the capital of Dominica, West Indies (W.I.), to the proud parents of Archibald and Margaret (Williams) Chambers. He is the youngest of seven siblings. At an early age, his family moved to another island called Montserrat, W.I. There he attended a Methodist School and later became a master carpenter making furnishings from trees in his carpentry shop.

As a young man, James relocated to England where he resided for about five years. In 1963, he came to America where he lived in the New York area. After some years, he became a father for the first time to his only son.

Life has a way of bringing many experiences into one's life; and he eventually journeyed to South Florida where he now resides. James is the proud grandfather of two grandchildren, one grandson and one granddaughter, and has many extended relatives and friends, all of whom he loves dearly.

James, an avid reader, has studied art, music, science, metaphysics, and several religious disciplines; he is also an ardent reader of history. James spends his leisure time at the beach, the park, gardening, and listening to music.

It has always been in his heart to paint and write, so it is his joy to share thoughts and ideas with you.

Enjoy the prose, short stories and paintings by James!